China

Julie McCulloch

www.heinemann.co.uk
Visit our website to find out more information about **Heinemann Library** books.

To order:
☎ Phone 44 (0) 1865 888066
▤ Send a fax to 44 (0) 1865 314091
💻 Visit the Heinemann Bookshop at www.heinemann.co.uk to browse our catalogue and order online.

First published in Great Britain by Heinemann Library, Halley Court, Jordan Hill, Oxford OX2 8EJ, a division of Reed Educational and Professional Publishing Ltd. Heinemann is a registered trademark of Reed Educational & Professional Publishing Limited.

OXFORD MELBOURNE AUCKLAND JOHANNESBURG BLANTYRE
GABORONE IBADAN PORTSMOUTH NH (USA) CHICAGO

Designed by Tinstar Design (www.tinstar.co.uk)
Illustrations by Nicholas Beresford-Davies
Originated by Dot Gradations
Printed by Wing King Tong in Hong Kong.

ISBN 0 431 11705 5   (hardback)   ISBN 0 431 11712 8   (paperback)
05 04 03 02   06 05 04 03 02
10 9 8 7 6 5 4 3 2   10 9 8 7 6 5 4 3 2 1

British Library Cataloguing in Publication Data
McCulloch, Julie
    China. – (A world of recipes)
    1. Cookery, Chinese – Juvenile literature 2. China –
    Description and travel – Juvenile literature
    I. Title
    641.5'123'0951

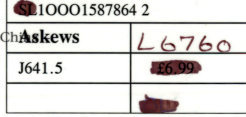

Acknowledgements
The Publishers would like to thank the following for permission to reproduce photographs:
Robert Harding, p.5; All other photographs by Gareth Boden

Our thanks to Sue Townsend, home economist, and Sue Mildenhall for their comments in the preparation of this book.

Every effort has been made to contact copyright holders of any material reproduced in this book. Any omissions will be rectified in subsequent printings if notice is given to the Publisher.

Words appearing in the text in bold, **like this**, are explained in the glossary.

Contents

Key

* easy

** medium

*** difficult

Chinese food

feet **HEIGHT** metres
feet		metres
over 13120		over 4000
6560-13120		2000-4000
3277-6557		1000-1999
1640-3277		500-999
656-1637		200-499
under 656		under 200

kilometres 0 150 300 450 600 750
miles 0 150 300 450

RUSSIA

MONGOLIA

CHINA

Harbin

Shenyang

Great Wall of China

Beijing

NORTH KOREA

Seoul

SOUTH KOREA

Huang He (Yellow River)

Plateau of Tibet

NEPAL

BHUTAN

BANGLADESH

INDIA

MYANMAR (BURMA)

VIETNAM

LAOS

Nanking

Shanghai

Wuhan

Chongqing

Chang Jiang (Yangtze River)

TAIWAN

Canton

Macao

HONG KONG

South China Sea

China is a huge country, as big as all the countries of Europe put together. About one fifth of all the people in the world live in China.

Chinese cooking is one of the oldest styles of cooking in the world. Most Chinese meals consist of rice, noodles or bread, served with several small vegetable or fish dishes. Meat is eaten in small quantities.

In the past

The first Chinese farmers lived in about 2000 BC. They grew millet, a type of grain, along the banks of the Yellow River. As farming spread and developed, people in the south of China began to grow rice.

4

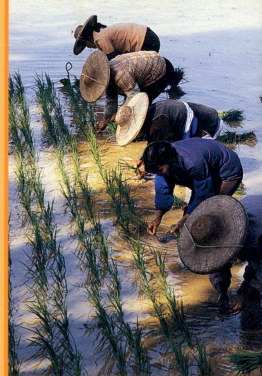

▶ Farmers in China planting out young rice plants.

In 221 BC, a huge wall, the Great Wall of China, was built to keep foreigners out of China. For thousands of years China was **isolated** from the rest of the world.

In the 16th century, traders from Portugal, Holland and Britain sailed to China. Since then, China has become more open, and Chinese cooking is popular in many countries.

Around the country

China's climate varies enormously between regions. In winter, the north of the country is very cold; in summer it is hot. The south is hot and **humid** for much of the year. Different crops grow in each area, which has led to each region specializing in different dishes.

The humid climate of southern China is ideal for growing rice. In the north, people grow wheat, millet and corn. In the eastern region, people eat a lot of fish and seafood. The western area specializes in hot, spicy food.

Chinese meals

Traditionally, breakfast in China is porridge made from rice, sometimes served with vegetables or bread. Lunch might be boiled rice with stir-fried vegetables, perhaps with a little meat. Supper is usually very like breakfast or lunch. Food is usually served on large plates in the middle of the table, and people help themselves.

Chinese people eat with chopsticks. Food is often cut up into bite-sized pieces so that it can easily be picked up. Using chopsticks is easy once you get the hang of it! See page 33 for easy-to-follow instructions.

Ingredients

spring onions

bean sprouts

water chestnuts

tofu

noodles

soy sauce

mushrooms

rice

cornflour

garlic

ginger

Chinese cooking uses quite simple ingredients – fresh vegetables, fish or meat, with a small amount of sauce to bring out their flavour.

Cornflour

Cornflour is used in China to thicken sauces. It is often used as part of a sauce called a **marinade**, as it helps the sauce coat the food. Cornflour is easy to buy.

Garlic

Garlic is used in many Chinese dishes. You can buy garlic in the vegetable section of most food shops or supermarkets.

Ginger

Fresh ginger is used in many Chinese dishes, usually **peeled** and **grated**, or finely **chopped**. Ginger is readily available in supermarkets. It is much better to use fresh rather than dried ginger, as its flavour is stronger.

Noodles

There are many different types of noodles in China. Some are made from wheat and egg, some from rice, and some from ground-up beans. The recipes in this book suggest using dried wheat and egg noodles. You should find these noodles, usually just called 'egg noodles', in packets in most supermarkets.

Oil

Chinese food is often cooked in sesame oil, made from sesame seeds. If you cannot find any, use vegetable oil instead for these recipes.

Rice

Rice is served with many Chinese dishes. It comes in two main types – short grain and long grain. Chinese people use long grain rice for most of their dishes.

Soy sauce

Soy sauce is made from soya beans, flour, salt and water. It is very salty, so you don't need to add any extra salt to your food if it contains soy sauce. You can find soy sauce in most supermarkets.

Tofu

Tofu is made from pulped soya beans. It is called 'doufu' in Chinese, but tofu in most countries. You can find tofu in most supermarkets.

Vegetables

Chinese cooking uses lots of fresh vegetables, some of which are more familiar outside China than others. The main vegetables used in the recipes in this book are bamboo shoots, bean sprouts, mushrooms, spring onions and water chestnuts. It is easy to buy fresh mushrooms and spring onions, but you may need to buy canned bamboo shoots, bean sprouts and water chestnuts.

Before you start

Kitchen rules

There are a few basic rules you should always follow when you are cooking.

- Ask an adult if you can use the kitchen.
- Some cooking processes, especially those involving hot water or oil, can be dangerous. When you see this sign, take extra care or ask an adult to help.
- Wash your hands before you start.
- Wear an apron to protect your clothes, and tie back long hair.
- Be very careful when you use sharp knives.
- Never leave pan handles sticking out in case you knock them.
- Always wear oven gloves to lift things in and out of the oven.
- Wash fruit and vegetables before you use them.

How long will it take?

Some of the recipes in this book are quick and easy, and some are more difficult and take longer. The strip across the top of the right hand page of each recipe tells you how long it takes to cook each dish from start to finish. It also shows how difficult each dish is to cook: every recipe is either * (easy), ** (medium) or *** (difficult).

Quantities and measurements

You can see how many people each recipe will serve at the top of the right hand page, too. Most of the recipes in this book make enough to feed two people. Where it is more sensible to make a larger amount, though, the recipe makes enough for four. You can multiply or divide the quantities if you want to cook for more or fewer people.

Ingredients for recipes can be measured in two ways. Metric measurements use grams and millilitres. Imperial measurements use ounces and fluid ounces. This book uses metric measurements. If you want to convert these into imperial measurements, see the chart on page 44.

In the recipes you will see the following abbreviations:

tbsp = tablespoon   g = grams
tsp = teaspoon   ml = millilitres

Utensils

To cook the recipes in this book, you will need these utensils (as well as kitchen essentials such as spoons, plates and bowls):

- chopping board
- colander
- double boiler
- food processor or blender
- frying pan
- grater
- heatproof bowl
- large, flat, ovenproof dish
- measuring jug
- saucepan with lid
- set of scales
- sharp knife
- **wok** (if you don't have a wok, you can use a large frying pan instead)
- wooden spoon

! Whenever you use kitchen knives, be very careful.

Mushroom and water chestnut soup

In China, soup is often served between courses. You could also eat this light soup as a starter or for lunch.

What you need

1 onion
100g mushrooms
50g canned water
   chestnuts
50g canned bamboo
   shoots
2 spring onions
1 vegetable stock cube
2 tbsp soy sauce

What you do

1 **Peel** the onion and finely **chop** it.

2 Cut the mushrooms into **slices**.

3 **Drain** the liquid from the canned water chestnuts and bamboo shoots.

4 Cut the tops and bottoms off the spring onions, and finely chop them.

5 Put 500ml water into a saucepan, and bring it to the **boil**. Crumble the stock cube into the water, and stir until it **dissolves**. Reduce the heat to a **simmer**.

6 Add the chopped onion and soy sauce to the stock. Simmer it for 10 minutes.

7 Add the sliced mushrooms and the drained water chestnuts and bamboo shoots. Simmer the soup for a further 5 minutes.

8 Carefully take the soup off the heat. Stir in the chopped spring onions.

MUSHROOMS

Over 300 different kinds of mushroom are grown in China! You could try experimenting with different types of mushroom in this dish. Some of the Chinese mushrooms you might be able to find in your local greengrocer's shop or supermarket are oyster mushrooms and shiitake mushrooms.

shiitake mushrooms

oyster mushrooms

Chinese scrambled eggs

People have kept chickens in China for thousands of years, and their eggs are used in many recipes. This simple dish is ideal as a snack or a light meal.

What you need

3 eggs
1 spring onion
1 tbsp soy sauce
1 tbsp vegetable oil

What you do

1 Crack the eggs into a small bowl. **Beat** them with a fork or a whisk until the yolk and the white are mixed.

2 Cut the top and bottom off the spring onion, and finely **chop** it.

3 Add the chopped spring onion and the soy sauce to the beaten eggs, and mix everything together well.

(!) 4 Heat the oil in a non-stick frying pan over a medium heat. Pour the egg mixture into the pan.

5 Stir the mixture gently with a wooden spoon until the eggs are just **set**. This should take about 3 minutes.

6 Serve the scrambled eggs at once.

ADDED EXTRAS

You could experiment by adding extra ingredients to your Chinese scrambled eggs. Try adding some sliced mushrooms or prawns at step 3 of the recipe.

Prawns with ginger sauce

This dish combines lots of typical Chinese flavours – seafood, ginger, soy sauce and vinegar. You need to allow 30 minutes for the prawns to **marinate** in the sauce before you cook them. If possible, use large prawns, such as tiger prawns. You can use frozen prawns, but **defrost** them completely by moving them from the freezer to the fridge at least 12 hours before using them.

What you need

small piece fresh
   ginger (about 2cm
   long)
2 tbsp soy sauce
1 tbsp vegetable oil
1 tbsp wine vinegar
   (red or white)
225g cooked peeled
   prawns, **thawed** if
   frozen
few sprigs fresh parsley

What you do

1 **Peel** the skin from the ginger, and **grate** or finely **chop** it.

2 Mix together the soy sauce, oil, wine vinegar and chopped ginger in an ovenproof dish.

3 Add the prawns, and stir them into the mixture so that they are well coated.

4 Leave the prawns to marinate for 30 minutes.

5 While the prawns are marinating, chop the parsley.

6 When the prawns have marinated, turn the grill on to a medium setting. Put the dish of marinated prawns under the grill.

7 **Grill** the prawns for 5 minutes, stirring them occasionally.

8 Put the grilled prawns onto plates, and sprinkle the parsley over them.

Chinese fish cakes

Fish cakes (or fish balls, as they are sometimes called) are very popular in China. Some can be **fried**, as shown here, others are **boiled** in water or stock. You could serve them with rice (see page 17) or noodles (see page 24). If you are using frozen fish fillets, make sure you **defrost** them completely by moving them from the freezer to the fridge at least 12 hours before you want to use them.

What you need

2 cod fillets, **thawed** if frozen
2 spring onions
1 clove garlic
1 tsp sugar
1 tsp soy sauce
2 tbsp vegetable oil
2 tbsp cornflour

What you do

1 Put the cod fillets into a food processor or blender. **Blend** them on a medium setting until they are in tiny pieces.

2 Cut the tops and bottoms off the spring onions, and finely **chop** them.

3 **Peel** the skin from the garlic clove, and finely chop it.

4 Put the blended fish, chopped spring onions and garlic into a bowl. Add the sugar, soy sauce and half the oil.

5 Using your fingers, mix everything together. Add about half the cornflour to bind the mixture together.

6 Sprinkle the rest of the cornflour onto a chopping board or work surface. Tip the fish cake mixture onto it and divide it into four pieces.

7 Gently shape each piece into a circle, coating the outside in cornflour.

8 Heat the rest of the oil in a non-stick frying pan over a medium heat. Add the fish cakes, and fry them for about 10 minutes, turning them occasionally to cook both sides.

9 Serve the fish cakes hot or cold.

PLAIN BOILED RICE

Many Chinese dishes are served with rice. This recipe makes enough plain boiled rice for 2 people (see also page 36).
1 Put 140g rice into a saucepan.
2 Add 400ml water
3 Bring to the boil, then **simmer** for 20 minutes, stirring occasionally, until the rice has soaked up all the water.

Stir-fried fish with mushrooms and cucumber

This recipe suggests using cod, but you could use other fish such as halibut or red snapper. If you're using frozen fish fillets, **defrost** them by moving them from the freezer to the fridge at least 12 hours before using them. Serve with plain boiled rice (see page 17).

What you need

2 cod fillets, **thawed** if frozen
2 tbsp soy sauce
2 tsp cornflour
1 small cucumber
40g mushrooms
1 clove garlic
small piece fresh ginger (about 2cm long)
2 tbsp vegetable oil
½ vegetable stock cube

What you do

1 Cut the cod fillets into pieces.

2 Mix together the soy sauce and the cornflour in a bowl. Add the cod pieces, and leave them to **marinate** for about an hour.

3 While the fish is marinating, cut the cucumber and mushrooms into **slices**.

4 **Peel** the skin from the garlic clove, and finely **chop** it.

5 Peel the skin from the ginger, and **grate** or finely chop it.

6 Put 150ml water into a saucepan, and bring it to the **boil**. Crumble the ½ stock cube into the water, and stir until it **dissolves**. Put the stock to one side.

7 When the fish has marinated, heat the oil in a **wok** or frying pan over a medium heat. Carefully put the fish pieces and the **marinade** into the wok.

8 Add the sliced mushrooms, cucumber pieces and the chopped garlic and ginger to the wok. **Stir-fry** for 2 minutes.

9 Add the vegetable stock. Reduce the heat, cook for 10 minutes, then serve.

19

Lemon chicken stir-fry

To make this dish, the chicken needs to be left to **marinate** in the lemon juice and soy sauce, so that it absorbs all their flavours. Try serving it with plain boiled rice (see page 17).

What you need

2 boneless chicken breasts
4 tbsp lemon juice
1 tbsp soy sauce
2 tsp cornflour
1 clove garlic
1 tbsp vegetable oil
50g canned water chestnuts
25g canned bamboo shoots

What you do

1 Take any skin off the chicken breasts and cut them into **slices**.

2 Mix together the soy sauce, the cornflour and 2 tbsp of the lemon juice in a bowl. Add the chicken, turning it several times so that it is well covered with the mixture.

3 Marinate the chicken for an hour, turning it occasionally.

4 While the chicken is marinating, **peel** the skin from the garlic, and finely **chop** it.

5 When the chicken has marinaded, heat the oil in a **wok** or frying pan over a medium heat. Add the chopped garlic, the chicken, and the marinade, and **stir-fry** for 7 minutes.

6 Add the water chestnuts, bamboo shoots and the rest of the lemon juice. Stir-fry for 3 minutes more, then serve.

VEGETARIAN VERSION

You could try making a **vegetarian** version of this dish by replacing the chicken with vegetables such as mushrooms or mange-tout peas.

21

Honey chicken

Honey or sugar are regularly used in savoury Chinese dishes. Chinese cooks feel that a small amount of sweet flavour helps balance the savoury or salty ingredients in a dish. Try serving this with plain boiled rice (see page 17).

What you need

small piece fresh ginger (about 2cm long)
2 boneless chicken breasts
1 tbsp vegetable oil
2 tbsp soy sauce
2 tbsp honey
2 spring onions

What you do

1 **Peel** the skin from the ginger, and **grate** or finely **chop** it.

2 Take any skin off the chicken breasts and cut them into **slices**.

⚠ **3** Heat the oil in a **wok** or frying pan over a medium heat. Add the chicken slices.

4 **Fry** the chicken slices for about 5 minutes, turning them occasionally.

5 In a bowl, mix together the soy sauce, 50ml water, the honey and chopped ginger, then carefully pour this mixture into the wok.

6 Bring the liquid in the pan to the **boil**, put the lid on and let it **simmer** for 10 minutes.

7 Cut the tops and bottoms off the spring onions, and finely chop them.

8 Stir them into the chicken mixture, then serve.

CHINESE SUGAR

Chinese cooks use two main types of sugar: brown slab sugar and rock candy. Brown slab sugar is pressed into hard, flat slabs and sold in fingers about 15cm long. Rock candy is a pale honey colour, and is sold in lumps that look like crystals. You might find some in oriental food shops.

Noodles with minced pork

This dish is called 'Mayi Hshang Shu' in Chinese, which means 'ants climbing a tree'. The minced pork is thought to look like ants climbing a tree when it is added to the noodles!

What you need

125g fine egg noodles
   (see page 25)
small piece fresh ginger
   (about 2cm long)
1 clove garlic
1 vegetable stock cube
1 tbsp vegetable oil
225g minced pork
2 tbsp soy sauce
2 tsp sugar
2 spring onions

What you do

1 Put the noodles into a large bowl. Pour over enough warm water to cover them, and leave them to soak for 15 minutes.

2 **Peel** the skin from the ginger, and **grate** or finely **chop** it.

3 Peel the skin from the garlic clove, and finely chop it.

4 Put 250ml water into a saucepan, and bring it to the **boil**. Crumble the stock cube into the water, and stir until it **dissolves**. **Cover** the pan, and put the stock to one side.

5 Heat the oil in a **wok** or frying pan over a medium heat. Add the minced pork, and **stir-fry** for 5 minutes, until the meat starts to go brown.

6 Add the chopped ginger and garlic, soy sauce, sugar and vegetable stock to the wok.

7 Carefully **drain** the noodles, and add them to the wok. Reduce the heat and **simmer** the mixture for about 15 minutes until most of the liquid has gone.

8 Cut the tops and bottoms off the spring onions, and finely chop them.

9 Spoon the pork and noodle mixture onto plates, and sprinkle the chopped spring onions over the top.

NOODLES

Egg noodles are made in different sizes – fine, medium and thick. They are sold in packets, telling you what size they are. Fine noodles are best for this dish, as they mix well with the minced pork. They are sometimes called 'thread noodles'.

Vegetable chow mein

This is a very simple noodle and vegetable dish. Medium egg noodles are the best (see page 25).

What you need

75g mushrooms

75g mange-tout

130g medium egg noodles

2 tbsp vegetable oil

75g canned bamboo shoots

3 tbsp soy sauce

What you do

1 Cut the mushrooms into slices.

2 Cut the tops and bottoms off the mange-tout.

3 Pour 25ml water into a pan and bring it to the **boil**. Add the noodles, and boil them for about 3 minutes, until they are just beginning to go soft.

4 Carefully tip the noodles into a colander, and rinse them in cold water.

5 **Drain** the water from the bamboo shoots by emptying them into a sieve or colander.

6 Heat the oil in a **wok** or frying pan. Add the sliced mushrooms, mange-tout and bamboo shoots, and **stir-fry** for 4 minutes.

(!) 7 Add the drained noodles and soy sauce, and stir-fry for about 5 minutes, until the noodles are hot, then serve.

NOODLES TO GO...

Tasty noodle dishes are served from food stalls all over China. Called 'xiao chi', which means 'small eats', they are eaten as snacks or quick meals.

Tofu stir-fry

Tofu tastes quite **bland** on its own, so it is usually cooked with other ingredients which add flavour. In this dish, it is **fried** with enough chilli powder to give it flavour, without making the dish too hot and spicy. If you don't like chilli, just leave it out.

What you need

1 onion
small piece fresh
   ginger (about 2cm
   long)
1 tbsp vegetable oil
100g tofu
½ tsp chilli powder
   (optional)
several leaves of pak
   choi, or other
   greens (see page 29)
1 tbsp soy sauce

What you do

1 **Peel** the skin from the onion, and finely **chop** it.

2 Peel the skin from the ginger, and **grate** or finely chop it.

3 Cut the tofu into cubes about 2cm across.

4 Heat the oil in a **wok** or frying pan over a medium heat. Add the cubed tofu, chopped ginger and chilli powder (if using), and fry for about 10 minutes, until the tofu is golden brown.

5 Add the chopped onion to the wok, and **stir-fry** for 3 minutes.

6 Cut the pak choi leaves in half. Add them and the soy sauce to the wok. Stir-fry for 2 minutes, until the pak choi leaves are just beginning to droop, then serve.

PAK CHOI

Pak choi is a type of Chinese cabbage. It is sometimes known as 'bok choy'. It has long white stems and green leaves. You can usually find pak choi in oriental food shops, and sometimes in supermarkets. If you can't find pak choi, you can replace it with fresh spinach in this dish.

Carrots with honey

Carrots are a popular vegetable in China. They are made into flower shapes to decorate dishes, and even carved into ornate sculptures, such as dragons, for **banquets**!

What you need

400g carrots
1 tbsp vegetable oil
1 tbsp honey
1 tbsp fresh coriander
   leaves
50g pine nuts
   (see page 31)

What you do

1 **Peel** the skin from the carrots, and carefully cut them into long, thin strips using a sharp knife.

2 Put the oil, 100ml water and the honey into a saucepan. Heat the mixture over a high heat until it comes to the **boil**.

3 Reduce the heat to medium. Add the carrots, then **cover** the pan and cook for 10 minutes.

4 While the carrots are cooking, finely **chop** the fresh coriander leaves.

5 Put the pine nuts into a frying pan without any oil. Turn the heat to medium and **toast** them for about 5 minutes, until they turn golden brown.

6 When the carrots are just beginning to soften, take the pan off the heat, and stir in the chopped coriander and pine nuts.

VEGETABLE VARIATIONS

You could try cooking other vegetables in this way. Green beans or mange tout work very well. They don't need to be cooked for as long as the carrots – you should boil them for about 3 or 4 minutes, rather than 10.

PINE NUTS

You should be able to buy pine nuts from most food shops and supermarkets. You can eat them raw, but they taste better if you toast them for a few minutes first.

31

Celery and prawn salad

Try serving this salad on its own or as a side dish.

What you need

2 stalks celery
2 spring onions
small piece fresh
    ginger (about 2cm
    long)
100g bean sprouts
    (fresh or canned)
50g cooked peeled
    prawns (**thawed** if
    frozen)
1 tbsp soy sauce
1 tbsp wine vinegar
    (red or white)
1 tbsp vegetable oil

What you do

1 Carefully cut the celery stalks into **slices** using a sharp knife.

2 Cut the tops and bottoms off the spring onions, and slice them.

3 **Peel** the skin from the ginger, and **grate** or finely **chop** it.

4 Wash the fresh bean sprouts by putting them into a sieve or colander, then rinsing them with cold water, or **drain** canned bean sprouts.

5 Put the chopped celery, spring onion, ginger, bean sprouts and prawns into a salad bowl.

6 Mix together the soy sauce, wine vinegar and oil in a small bowl to make a **dressing** for the salad.

7 Pour the dressing over the salad. Mix everything together, and serve.

HOW TO USE CHOPSTICKS

Pick up one chopstick, and hold it between your thumb and first two fingers. This chopstick is the one that will move.

Put the second chopstick between your second and third fingers, and behind your thumb. This chopstick stays still. Move the top chopstick up and down with your thumb and first finger so that the tips of the chopsticks meet.

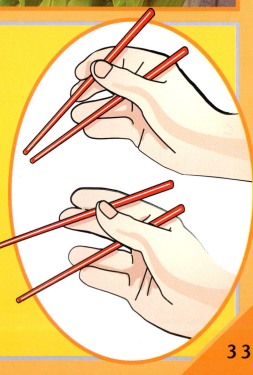

Ginger and spring onion noodles

This noodle dish is an ideal accompaniment for some of the main dishes in this book, such as lemon chicken stir-fry (page 20), honey chicken (page 22) and tofu stir-fry (page 28).

What you need

2 spring onions
small piece fresh ginger (about 2cm long)
130g medium egg noodles
1 tbsp vegetable oil
1 tbsp soy sauce

What you do

1 Cut the tops and bottoms off the spring onions, and finely **chop** them.

2 **Peel** the skin from the ginger, and **grate** or finely chop it.

3 Bring a pan of water to the **boil**. Carefully add the noodles, and boil them for about 3 minutes, until they are just beginning to go soft.

4 Tip the noodles into a colander to **drain** them, then put them back into the pan. Reduce the heat to low.

5 Add the chopped spring onions, chopped ginger, oil and soy sauce.

6 Stir everything together and cook for another 2 minutes.

SPRING ONIONS

Spring onions, also known as scallions, are used in many Chinese dishes. They have a milder flavour than ordinary onions, and they cook very quickly. This makes them ideal for **stir-fries** and other dishes that need to be cooked quickly. The green stems of the spring onions are sometimes shredded or curled into flower shapes to decorate dishes.

Three rice dishes

Here are three different ways of cooking rice to accompany your Chinese meal – coconut rice, rice with peas and egg fried rice. You could also serve plain boiled rice – see the box on page 17 for how to cook this.

What you need

Coconut rice
Ready to eat: 25 minutes
140g rice
500ml coconut
    milk

Rice with peas
Ready to eat: 25 minutes
140g rice
140g frozen peas
1 tbsp soy sauce

Egg fried rice
Ready to eat: 30 minutes
140g rice
2 tbsp vegetable oil
2 eggs

What you do

Coconut rice

1 Put the rice into a saucepan and add the coconut milk.

2 Bring to the **boil**, then **cover** the pan and **simmer** for 20 minutes, stirring occasionally.

Rice with peas

1 Put the rice and peas into a saucepan and add 400ml water.

2 Bring to the boil, then cover the pan and simmer for 20 minutes, stirring occasionally.

3 Sprinkle the rice with the soy sauce before serving.

Egg fried rice

1 Cook the rice on its own as described in the recipes on page 36.

2 Crack the eggs into a small bowl. **Beat** them with a fork or a whisk until the yolk and the white are mixed.

⊙ **3** Heat the oil in a non-stick frying pan over a medium heat. Add the beaten eggs, and **fry**, stirring all the time, for about 4 minutes.

4 Add the cooked rice to the frying pan, and mix well with the egg.

Egg fried rice

Rice with peas

Coconut rice

Sweet chestnut balls

Chestnuts have been used in Chinese cooking for thousands of years. These sweet chestnut balls are eaten in China as a dessert or a snack.

What you need

200g canned
    chestnuts
3 tbsp set honey
40g icing sugar
1 tsp cinnamon

What you do

1 If the chestnuts are in liquid in the can, **drain** them by pouring the chestnuts into a colander or sieve and patting them dry with paper towel.

2 Put the chestnuts and the honey into a food processor or blender. **Blend** together on the highest setting.

3 Put the icing sugar and cinnamon into a bowl, and mix them together with a spoon.

4 Using your fingers, take a little of the chestnut and honey paste out of the food processor or blender. Roll it into a ball.

5 Cover the ball in sugar and cinnamon by rolling it in the mixture in the bowl.

6 Repeat steps 4 and 5 with the rest of the chestnut and honey paste.

7 Serve the sweet chestnut balls straight away, or keep them in the fridge until you are ready to eat them.

ROAST CHESTNUTS

Roast chestnuts are served all over China. In autumn, chestnut sellers set up stalls on the streets of many Chinese cities, where they roast chestnuts over charcoal.

Chocolate lychees

Lychees are a **tropical** fruit. Originally, they came from southern China, but now people grow them in many tropical countries. They have a very sweet taste, and a texture a bit like jelly. Chocolate-coated lychees make a sweet snack.

What you need

80g plain chocolate
200g canned lychees (or fresh lychees, if available. You need to peel them so add about 10 minutes to the '**Ready to eat**' time.)

What you do

1 Before you start cooking, you need to find a heatproof bowl that fits on top of your saucepan. Or you can melt the chocolate in the microwave in a non-metallic, microwave proof bowl.

2 Break the chocolate into pieces and put into the bowl. Either cook on medium power in the microwave for 1 minute and stir until melted. Carry on from step 7.

3 Or put 400ml water into the saucepan. Heat the water over a medium heat until just bubbling at the edges, but not **boiling**. Reduce the heat to low.

4 Put the bowl of chocolate on top of the pan without letting it touch the hot water. Leave until the chocolate melts (probably about 5 minutes).

5 While the chocolate is melting, **drain** the liquid from the canned lychees by pouring them into a sieve or colander. Pat them dry with paper towel.

⚠ 6 Turn off the heat. Using oven gloves, take the bowl of melted chocolate from the top of the pan.

7 Pick up a lychee, and dip one half of it into the melted chocolate. Put the lychee onto a sheet of greaseproof paper. (Use a cocktail stick to help pick up the lychee if you need to.)

8 Repeat step 7 with all the lychees.

9 Put the chocolate-coated lychees to **chill** in the fridge for about an hour to let the chocolate harden, then serve.

Orange tea

Chinese people have grown and drunk tea for thousands of years. This recipe suggests using oranges to make a sweet tea that is served at the end of a meal. You could try grapefruit or canned pineapple. Have fun experimenting!

What you need

2 oranges
1 tbsp cornflour
50g sugar

What you do

1 **Peel** the oranges, then **chop** them into small pieces.

2 Put the cornflour and sugar into a saucepan. Add 400ml water.

3 Put the saucepan over a medium heat, and bring the mixture to the **boil**, stirring all the time.

4 Add the orange pieces.

5 Reduce the heat to medium and **simmer** the tea for another 5 minutes. Drink with care as it will be hot!

DIFFERENT TEAS

Many different types of tea are produced in China. Different areas of the country produce different flavour teas. Some of the Chinese teas you might be able to find in shops and supermarkets include:

● 'oolong': a smooth, fruity, slightly spicy tea

● 'lapsang souchong': a strongly flavoured tea, in which the leaves are smoked to give a smoky smell and flavour

● 'gunpowder': a tea made from greyish tea leaves

Further information

Here are some places to find out more about Chinese cooking.

Books

Cooking the Chinese way
Ling Yu, Lerner, 1983

Food and recipes of China
Theresa M. Beatty, Powerkids, 1999

Food in China
Jennifer Tan, Rourke Publishing Group, 1989

A Visit to China
Peter & Connie Roop, Heinemann Library, 1998

Websites

www.belgourmet.com/sitegb/index.html
www.uk.chopstix.net/recipes/index.html
www.astray.com/recipes/?search=chinese
www.bitesofasia.com/home.html
www.yumyum.com/recipes.htm

Conversion chart

Ingredients for recipes can be measured in two different ways. Metric measurements use grams and millilitres. Imperial measurements use ounces and fluid ounces. This book uses metric measurements. The chart here shows you how to convert measurements from metric to imperial.

SOLIDS		LIQUIDS	
METRIC	IMPERIAL	METRIC	IMPERIAL
10g	¼ oz	30ml	1 fl oz
15g	½ oz	50ml	2 fl oz
25g	1 oz	75ml	2½ fl oz
50g	1¾ oz	100ml	3½ fl oz
75g	2¾ oz	125ml	4 fl oz
100g	3½ oz	150ml	5 fl oz
150g	5 oz	300ml	10 fl oz
250g	9 oz	600ml	20 fl oz

Healthy eating

This diagram shows which foods you should eat to stay healthy. Most of your food should come from the bottom of the pyramid. Eat some foods from the middle every day. Only eat a little of the foods from the top.

Healthy eating, Chinese style

Many Chinese dishes are served with rice or noodles, which belong to the bottom of the pyramid. In China, people eat some meat and fish, as well as tofu, which is made from soybeans. They also use lots of fresh vegetables, so you can see how healthy Chinese cooking is!

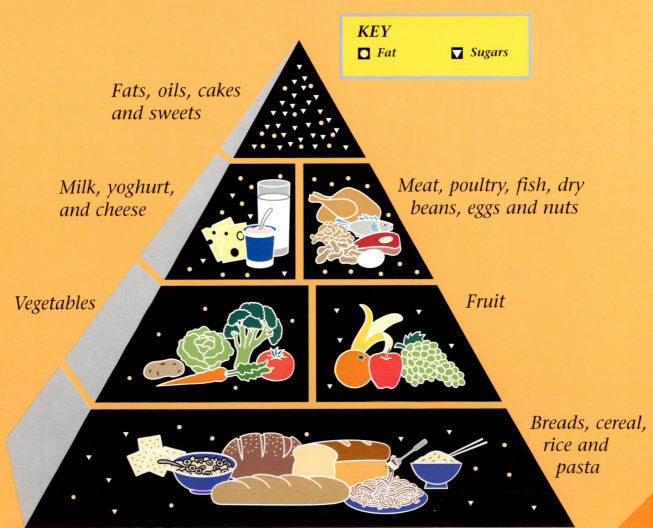

KEY
◻ Fat   ▽ Sugars

Fats, oils, cakes and sweets

Milk, yoghurt, and cheese

Meat, poultry, fish, dry beans, eggs and nuts

Vegetables

Fruit

Breads, cereal, rice and pasta

Glossary

banquets grand meals served on special occasions, usually with lots of courses

beat mix something together strongly, such as egg yolks and whites

bland without much flavour

blend mix ingredients together in a blender or food processor

boil cook a liquid on the hob. Boiling liquid bubbles and steams strongly.

chill put a dish in the fridge for several hours before serving

chop cut something into pieces using a knife

cover put a lid on a pan, or foil over a dish

defrost allow something that is frozen to thaw

dissolve mix something, such as sugar, until it disappears into a liquid

drain remove liquid, usually by pouring something into a colander or sieve

dressing cold sauce for a salad

fry cook something in oil in a pan

grate break something, such as cheese, into small pieces using a grater

grill cook something under the grill

humid a mixture of heat and moisture in the climate

isolated cut or separated off from other people or places

marinate soak something, such as meat or fish, in a mixture called a **marinade** before cooking, so that it absorbs the taste of the mixture

peel remove the skin of a fruit or vegetable

set food, such as jelly or eggs, that is not liquid any more is called set

simmer cook a liquid on the hob. Simmering liquid bubbles and steams gently.

slice cut something into thin, flat pieces

stir-fry fry something very quickly in a wok or frying pan, stirring all the time

thaw defrost something which has been frozen

toast in this book, cook something in a pan without any oil in it

tropical a place with a hot, wet climate is said to be tropical

vegetarian food that does not contain any meat or fish. People who don't eat meat are called vegetarians.

wok a round, deep pan used for cooking many Chinese dishes

Index